Gus Did It

Written by
Stephen Rickard

Illustrated by
Maarten Lenoir

Pick up the sock.

Pick up the cap.

Pick up the dog.
Tip it on the rug.

Pick up the cup.

Tip it in the sack.

Get the mop.

Gus did it!

Gus is not sad.

Hide and Peek

Written by
Cath Jones

Illustrated by
Ekaterina Anfilova

Duck woke up feeling very happy. Today was her birthday.

Lots of the animals came to visit Duck.

"Happy birthday, Duck," said Chicken and Sheep.

"Would you like to play hide and seek?" Owl asked.

"Oh yes!" said Duck. "Hide and seek is the best game ever! Let's play it!"